COLLEGE + UNIVERSITY SUCCESS

201 Tips From A Professor

Brian Harris, B.A., M.Ed.

ISBN 9781791996819

CGS Communications, Inc.
www.cgscommunications.com

HOW TO BE A SUCCESSFUL COLLEGE/UNIVERSITY STUDENT

A significant number of students never complete their college or university education. This book is intended to help you to be one of the graduating students.

For more than 20 years I was the Department Head of Guidance in several high schools. I have also taught part-time at several colleges and universities. These experiences have given me firsthand knowledge to help me write this book to assist you to be more successful in college/university.

While my experience as a high school counsellor gave me some great insights into why students choose certain college and university programs, my experiences in working in colleges and universities gives me a strong understanding of what students have to do to be successful.

As previously stated, the intent of this

book is to help you to be more successful at college or university, to help you to be one of the graduating students. It has been said that success leaves clues. In this book I will present some of the clues and some of the practical strategies and tips that I have seen students use to be more successful.

Rather than provide an essay style format to give my observations, I have chosen to present the tips and strategies in short one sentence bites of information. This format allows you to read a page or two at your own convenience. You can even pick up the book and start in the middle if you wish, or for the really creative, you can start at the end of the book and work backwards.

The manner in which you read this book is not as important as finding a few tips and strategies that you can actually use to help make a positive difference in your studies. Every tip in this book is not intended for every student. It is up to you to explore and find some tips in this book that can help you to be more successful.

The tips in this book could be grouped

(although they aren't) into 7 categories. The categories that contribute to being a successful university student are as follows:

i) Choose a program that builds on your strengths.

ii) Find a healthy balance between your social life and your academic studies.

iii) Success favours those who are prepared.

iv) Understand the difference between high school and college/university.

v) Know where to get help.

vi) Have a reason to succeed.

vii) Believe that you can succeed.

Before providing 201 tips to help you to be more successful, I would like to provide a few thoughts on each of the 7 factors listed above. This can help you to better understand the tips that you will be looking at in the remainder of this book.

i) CHOOSE A PROGRAM THAT BUILDS ON YOUR STRENGTHS

One of the most important contributors to being successful in anything that you do is to build on your strengths. Marcus Buckingham, in his bestselling book *Go Put Your Strengths To Work* states, "A little less than two out of ten people succeed in capitalizing on their strengths. And as the research reveals, those two people are significantly more productive. Your strengths magnify you."

The most successful businesses build on their employee's strengths. For example, at Toyota all new managers must attend a three day Great Manager program that shows them how to spot the strengths of the people they supervise. At Yahoo, all new managers are required to take an online survey that measures their talents and pinpoints their strengths.

In working with high school students for over 20 years, I stressed the importance of choosing a college/university program that was based on their strengths. Your strengths are a combination of your interests and your abilities (and your values).

Let me provide a few examples of what I am talking about. Derrick was a university student who struggled during his first semester of studies. He was in a science program, largely due to his perception that this was an area that might help him get a good job when he graduated. Derrick was unsuccessful because his program was not based on his interests and his abilities. In high school, Derrick's real love was English and to be more precise, creative writing. In addition to this being Derrick's strongest interest in high school, it was also the subject where he achieved his highest marks.

In other words, English (and creative writing) was an area that was Derrick's strength because it was based on both his interests and abilities. It was also based on his values because he believed that writers could make an important contribution to our world. After a dismal first term in university, Derrick changed his program emphasis to English where he instantly enjoyed great success.

Confucius said, "Find a job that you love, and you will never have to work a day in your life." The same is true in college or university.

Find a program that you love (and that you do well), and your studies will be much more pleasurable (and successful) for you.

Interestingly, most people think that the key to success is working on their weaknesses. In reality, the opposite is true. In a 2001 poll, only 41% of Americans chose building on their strengths as the key to success while in the UK and Canada, this percentage dropped to 38%, and in Japan and China, only 24% of the people surveyed believed that success came from building on their strengths. Success is best attained by building on your strengths, but if you believe that success is best attained by focussing on your weaknesses, you might expend a great amount of effort in your studies, but still be unsuccessful.

The truth is that you will be more successful in your studies (and in your future occupation) when you focus on what you love to do and what you do best.

Nicole enjoyed the study of languages; she also loved to play the piano. When she chose her college program, she decided to study languages. In spite of passing grades after first year, Nicole never returned back to college for her second year of studies. Success in isn't always about ability. Nicole had the ability to be successful in languages at college, but when asked why she decided not to return back to college after her first year of studies, she said, "My heart wasn't in what I was doing."

After taking a year off, Nicole then returned back to college to study music. This time, she was incredibly successful and very happy. Playing the piano was Nicole's love. This is what she did best, and this is what gave her great pleasure. Nicole eventually graduated from college, having a very successful experience, and she went on to have an equally successful career in the music industry.

Not only should your program be based on your strengths (your interests and abilities), but most of the courses you choose within your program should also be based on your strengths. Before you register for your classes at the beginning of a school year, it makes a lot of sense to look at all the courses that are available to you in your program of studies. Ask yourself: "Which courses do I have to take? Which courses are optional for me? Which courses will build on my abilities and interests?" Read the course descriptions and if possible, consult with other students who have taken the courses. You can also schedule an appointment within the Department of your main interests to talk to a Faculty member about your course selections.

When you build on your strengths you will be more optimistic about school. If you do encounter any obstacles you will be more resilient in facing them and overcoming them.

When you build on your strengths, you will feel better about yourself. You will be happier. You will be more confident. You will be more successful.

ii) FIND A HEALTHY BALANCE BETWEEN YOUR SOCIAL LIFE AND YOUR ACADEMIC STUDIES

There is no doubt that a significant number of students who are unsuccessful have spent too much time "having fun" and too little time in their actual studies.

As a high school counselor I often invited former graduates from our school who were now in college or university to return back to our high school to talk to our students about their experiences. When I first started doing this, I became aware that some students enjoyed talking about the parties, the bars, and in general all the fun they were having. Other students talked more about their courses. After a few years of being involved in this activity, I decided to conduct an informal survey of how what a college or university student emphasized affected their actual success.

Although this was an informal study, based on approximately 125 students, here is what I found. Ninety-one percent of the students (now in college or university) who talked primarily about their courses and their learning successfully completed their first year of studies. On the other hand, only 43% of the students who focussed on talking about the parties and their great social life were successful at the end of their first year.

Of additional interest, of the 9% of the serious students who were not successful, in follow up interviews with several of these students, I discovered that many of them were doing very well up until their final exams when either stress or an illness sidelined them. It is possible that these students might have failed to have some non-academic activities in their life. While the main purpose of college or university is to learn, there is still a need to have some fun.

In my experience, students who quickly adapt to college/university life and enjoy their courses are those who get involved in some way: whether it's through a club, a team, volunteer work, or some other form of campus activity. I often hear successful students talking about being a part of orientation activities that helped them to feel more comfortable on campus. Such activities often have the added bonus of helping students to make new friends.

I am sometimes asked if there is a recommended ratio between "studying" and "playing". In other words, what students are asking is something along the lines of "Should I spend 80% of my time focussing on my course requirements and 20% of my time doing something other than my course work?" I don't have an answer to this question, at least not an answer that provides specific percentages. What I would say though is that the greatest amount of your time should be spent focussing on attending your classes, completing your homework, preparing for your next day's classes, and preparing for future tests and assignment. Having said this, there is a need to spend at least an hour or two each day having fun with your friends and/or being involved in some form of recreational activity (even if it's just going for a walk; and better yet, going for a walk with a friend).

One of the most important aspects of achieving a balance in your life is getting enough sleep. Consider the following facts from the National Sleep Research Project in Australia:

- 17 hours of sustained wakefulness leads to a decrease in performance

- exposure to noise at night can suppress the immune function even if the sleeper doesn't wake up

- unfamiliar noise during the first two hours
of sleep and the last two hours
have the greatest disruption
on the sleep cycle

    - teenagers need as much sleep
as small children (10 hours a night)

    - as a group, 18-24 year-olds who are
deprived of sleep suffer more from
impaired performance than older adults

Getting enough sleep can make a positive difference in helping you to be successful at university because it helps you to perform at your highest level and also helps to prevent you from getting sick.

Having said this, consider the above facts from the National Sleep Project once again. If you are living away from home while you are attending college/university, it might be more difficult for you to adjust to your new surroundings and get a good night's sleep. In addition, due to possible noises around you, your sleep cycle might be affected leaving you feeling tired and resulting in performing at a lower level. Finally, if you regularly stay awake for more than 17 hours at a time (for whatever reason), this will lead to a decrease in performance. It is a common practice for some students to study well into the early morning before exams. The lack of sleep from such studying habits can lead to a decreased performance on your exams.

In addition to getting enough sleep, it is important each day to have some kind of physical release. This could include walking, swimming, jogging, riding a bike, yoga, and so on. The key factor here is that exercise helps to reduce stress. Allowing stress to build in your body over weeks and even months, paired together with poor sleep habits, will cause reduced performance which could have a detrimental affect on your assignments and exams (and your health).

Another important aspect of having a positive balance in your life is to eat (and drink) healthy. The first rule of good eating is to have a healthy nutritious breakfast. Unfortunately some university students tend to get up at the last minute and have nothing more than a coffee or soda for breakfast. This is not healthy, nor is snacking on junk food throughout the day. We all know these things, but for some students it's easier (and quicker) to eat foods that they know are unhealthy than it is to take the time to eat properly. Peak success requires attention to what you eat and drink.

Finally, in order to have a more positive balance in your life, you might have to learn to say no. With so many clubs and other activities, it's easy to get overinvolved. It might also be easy to promise a friend that you will do something for them. Saying yes to everyone else can leave you exhausted. You are attending college/university to increase your skills and knowledge. This can be difficult to accomplish if you are too tired to complete your assignments or study because you are spending too much time meeting the needs of others. Sometimes in order to achieve a balance in your life, you need to be selfish; you need to learn to say no.

Another significant aspect of finding balance in your life is to prioritize what you have to do. If you want to be one of the graduating students at your college/university (and I hope this is your goal), then you need to spend your greatest time and your best efforts in tasks directly related to successfully completing your courses. This means that attending all your classes should be a number one priority. Spending a specific amount of time each day to review your notes from that day as well as completing any assignments or readings for the next day should be high on your priority list. Success expert Stephen Covey said, "The key is not to prioritize what is on your schedule, but to schedule your priorities."

iii) SUCCESS FAVOURS THOSE WHO ARE PREPARED

It's been said that the harder you work, the luckier you will get. Another way of saying this is that success comes most often to those who have prepared for it.

Geoff Colvin in his bestselling book *Talent Is Overrated* states, "The factor that explains the most about great performance is something researchers call deliberate practice. Deliberate practice is hard. It hurts. But it works. More of it equals better performance. Tons of it equals great performance."

It might be more fun to do something other than attend all your classes. It might be more fun to do something other than your readings each day. It might be more fun to do something other than preparing study notes each day after class. It might even be more fun to daydream (or text, or surf the internet) than pay attention in class and record lecture notes. But, if you want to be successful in college/university (or in anything else in life), there are times when hard work is necessary.

Colvin's research goes a step further than just emphasizing hard work. The previous quote from his book talks about something called "deliberate practice". The best athletes or top musicians in the world don't just spend more hours practicing; they spend more hours of deliberate practice. Deliberate practice could be defined as practicing what is most important to be successful.

A professional golfer who wants to be more successful doesn't just spend more hours playing golf each day; he or she spends this time carefully working on a specific aspect of his/her game that will contribute to being more successful. Applying this principle to college/university success, you will not necessarily be more successful just because you attend all your classes or just because you spend hours each day looking at your texts. To be successful, you need to engage in what is termed "deliberate practice".

Deliberate practice means that when you are in class, you are fully engaged in the learning by participating whenever possible by answering or even asking questions, by taking careful notes that highlight what is most important, and by preparing before the class to already have some knowledge and other background information related to the lecture. To do this while your friends might be having fun can be hard work. To do this when you are tired (or bored) can be hard work. But this is an example of deliberate practice. This is the type of preparation that leads to success. This is the type of preparation that leads to what some would call "good luck". Thomas Jefferson said, "I'm a great believer in luck, and I find that the harder I work the more I have of it."

Some students spend hours and hours studying, only to fail their exams. In talking with these students, I often discovered that their definition of studying is reading their text or notes over and over again (sometimes even with one eye on the TV, or both ears on their favourite music). While this may approach may be an example of working hard, it is not an example of working smart. Deliberate practice requires you to do the things that will help you to be more successful. It is not just about spending more time. I could go out on a golf course and practice twelve hours a day and never improve my game unless my practice is based on doing the things that will actually make a difference in my game.

Research in the area of studying would tell you that simply reading your notes and text (regardless of how many hours you do this) is not going to help you to be as successful as actually forming questions that might be asked (from noting questions that your professor asks in class or even from old tests that might be stored in the college/university library) and then writing your answers to these questions (using your notes and text to help you).

Another simple technique is to make "study cards". An easy way to do this is to purchase small file cards. Use a different colour for each of your classes. Each day after class, form a list of questions based on the class lectures (and related text references). On one side of each file card, write your questions. On the backs of each file card, write your answers. By doing this daily, you will have a complete set of study cards when exam time arrives. You won't need to waste time creating new cards; they will already be done for you. This is an example of studying in a manner that will help to increase your success. This is an example of deliberate practice. Most importantly, this is an example of success favouring those who are prepared.

Some students find it helpful to study in a group with other students. This has the advantage of helping you to look at the course content from different perspectives. The kind of questions you thought might be on the exam might be different than those of another student. Study groups can help you to ensure that you haven't missed any key concepts within the course. They can help to reinforce your learning in a fun way. If you are going to form a study group, challenge yourself to work with the best students you can gather together. It has been said that we become the average of the five people we spend most of our time with; strive to spend your time with other students who want to be successful (and who have a proven record of being successful).

If you believe that your study skills are weak, ask your professor or teaching assistant for help. There are generally on-campus workshops that focus on helping students to improve their study skills.

Being prepared is not just about paying attention in class or engaging in meaningful study; it is also about how you prepare for your classes. You should have a course outline or a syllabus. Your course outline provides you with an overview of the topics you will be studying and it also provides the order in which you will study them (and often has the related dates as well).

Your learning in any class can be tremendously enhanced when you prepare for your classes by reading and even researching related materials for the topic of your next class. To already have some background information about what the professor is going to be teaching can help to increase your learning. In addition, it can help you to contribute in a meaningful way to class discussions and it can also help you to identify any new concepts that you don't understand so that you can ask questions of clarification in class.

Waiting until the night before your exams before trying to clarify anything you don't understand is not going to contribute to being successful.

Another important aspect of being prepared is related to how you organize your time. Throughout this book there are some tips on time management. For now, one of the most important aspects of managing your time (which really means managing yourself) is to have an agenda (whether in a book form or in a digital form on your computer or cell phone) where you record every assignment, every test, and every other commitment that you have in your life. This agenda should include clear notations as to due dates and what is expected for any assignments, projects or tests. Each day after your classes, it is critical that you review your agenda as you decide what you are going to do for your homework. When you have multiple upcoming assignments/tests it is important to prioritize what you have to do, and that you set a schedule that you can follow that will take you step-by-step to completing your work.

Leaving assignments and studying for tests at the last minute can be overwhelming and can result in poor marks (and create stress for you). My experience with college/university students tells me that a significant number of students fail courses in their first year because they waited until the last minute to complete major assignments or to study for exams. The way you organize yourself can directly contribute to being more successful in college/university.

iv) UNDERSTAND THE DIFFERENCES BETWEEN HIGH SCHOOL AND COLLEGE/UNIVERSITY

When I was a high school guidance counselor, a common question that students asked me was, "How is college/university different than high school?" As a college/university professor, I often heard students say, "This is so different than high school." How is college/university different than high school, and how can your understanding of these differences help you to be more successful?

For many years, as the Head of various high school guidance departments, I received a print-out of the final marks for all our former students from the various colleges and universities they now attended (this rarely happens anymore because of privacy laws). The main reason for receiving these marks was to help high school teachers better understand how their assessment of students compared to what actually happened in university. The reality was that most first year college/university students suffered a mark drop, on average, of about 10-15%. In other words, first year college/university students found that their marks, on average, were 10-15% lower than what they experienced in high school.

There are a few reasons that contribute to this decrease in marks. By understanding these reasons, you have a better chance of maintaining your high school mark average (or even improving it) throughout college/university.

First of all, one of the major differences between high school and college/university is that you will now be much more independent. For example, if you live in a campus residence or in some form of student housing, you will now be making your own daily decisions without the influence of your parents. This can include (but is not limited to) what you are going to eat, what time you wake up, what time you go to bed, whether you go to your classes, how you spend your free time, whether you do your homework, and so on. Students who have developed good success habits during high school will often continue these in college/university, especially if these habits are the result of being self-motivated instead of constantly being "pushed" by a parent or teacher. On the other hand, students with poor work habits and/or who depended on their parents to remind them when assignments were due, etc. may find the sudden independence leading to a lack of success.

In college/university, much more than high school, you will find that you are in charge of more aspects of your life. If you recognize this, and attempt to make wise decisions for yourself (based on many of the tips and strategies in this book), you can be successful. Not only can you enjoy academic success, but you can also achieve a greater sense of confidence as you establish yourself as a person, independent from your parents.

Another difference between high school and college/university is your relationship with your teachers. In high school, successful students often establish a close bond with their teachers. Given that high school classes tend to be much smaller in size than college/university classes, your high school teachers generally knew you by your first name. In addition, as a result of participating on teams and in clubs (where your teachers may be your coaches and/or staff advisors), you often develop strong rapport with your teachers.

For many students, the "bond" that they formed with their high school teachers and the comfort of being in a smaller class contributed strongly to their success. Suddenly in college/university where classes in your first two years are often over 50 students (and some might even be over 100 students), it is more difficult to establish a bond with a professor. In addition, some students find it much harder in a large class to get involved in discussions (and the reality is that in some very large classes, there may be little discussion).

Having said this, there are still ways you can create a positive relationship with your professors that can make your learning more enjoyable and help you to be more successful.

Most professors are not likely going to be starting their classes by taking attendance and by trying to learn the names of their students. Therefore, it is your responsibility to find a way to introduce yourself to your professor. Whenever you answer a question in class, remind your professor of your name. Whenever your professor teaches a strong lesson, compliment him or her. If you have questions about an assignment, make an appointment to see your professor in person (be sure to prepare some specific questions so you don't waste the professor's time).

As you create a relationship between you and the professor, this will help to make your class more enjoyable and it will also create some rapport between the two of you which could be helpful if you need some individual feedback on what you might do to improve your marks if you ever have this need. Note as well, you can take this same approach with any teaching assistants who are involved with your classes.

Another excellent way to establish a positive relationship with a professor is to apply/ volunteer to assist with any research projects that your professor might be involved with.

A big difference between high school and college/university relates to your attendance. In many high schools, if you miss a class your parents would receive a telephone call or an email from the school alerting them of your absence. In addition, your teacher would keep a daily record of whether you were in class, or not. There is this constant expectation in high school for you to be attending your classes. This generally changes in college/university. In many classes, no attendance is even taken. No one is going to chase you (or contact your parents) if you miss any classes. Some students respond to this freedom by missing classes if they have something better to do, or if the class is boring or too hard. It doesn't take too many missed classes before you might find yourself in academic trouble. If you want to be successful in college/university, it is your responsibility to attend all your classes (and to be there on time).

Another difference between high school and college/university is the amount of expected work you are required to do out of class. From my experience, most high school students do the homework that has been assigned to them, but tend to do no homework if nothing has been assigned. This changes in college/university. As a rule of thumb, to be successful in university, you should be doing at least an hour of work outside of class for every hour you spend in class. And most important, you should be doing this work even if you have not been assigned any homework. As mentioned earlier, successful students review their lessons every day, highlighting important points in their notes, preparing study notes, completing related readings, and preparing for their next class.

Another difference between high school and college/university is that in high school you generally have the same classes each day. In college/university, you might only have a class in a certain subject area once a week, and you might even have a day or possibly two where you don't have any classes. Generally, your college/university classes will be much longer than your high school classes. As a result of what I have said so far, consider the reality that when you miss one college/university class it is similar to missing a complete week of work in high school. Taking this a step further, if you miss four college/university classes, this would be similar to missing a month of work in high school. I have seen some college/university students miss three or four classes, and then wonder why they are struggling to pass. Success is often very directly related to attending all your classes.

Success is definitely directly proportional to your own self-discipline as it relates to attendance and completing your work. No one is going to do it for you. It is unlikely that anyone is going to give you a "push" if you need it. Success in college/university, similar to success in your eventual career, comes from being self-motivated. For many students, this is the biggest difference between high school and college/university. You are completely responsible for your success or your lack of success; the sooner you realize this and take control of your life, the sooner you will experience success at college/university.

Having more freedom at college/university can also expose you to decisions that you have to make related to sex, drugs and alcohol. Poor decisions in any of these areas could lead to negative consequences in your personal life as well as impacting your success.

There are definitely some differences between high school and college/university.

These differences can be positive or they can be negative depending on your attitude and your level of self-discipline. The development of will-power and self-control will contribute to success throughout your life. Winners develop certain habits; self-discipline is one of them.

Jesse Owens, the four-time Olympic gold medalist, said, "We all have dreams. But in order to make dreams come into reality, it takes an awful lot of determination, dedication, self-discipline, and effort." In becoming successful, you would do well to master the traits that Owens identifies.

Here is a list of some other differences between high school and college/university that I have heard students talk about. College/university provides:

- greater opportunities to form new friendships with people from around the world

- the opportunity to build stronger friendships with others (after all, you are often with them 24/7)

- the opportunity to take a wider range of courses

- the opportunity to study more in-depth courses in your major area of interest

- the opportunity to become involved in research related to your major interest

- the opportunity to join a wider range of clubs or teams

- the opportunity to learn from experts in your field of studies

- the opportunity to form connections with people from around the world (connections that may be someday very important to you in your career)

- the opportunity to have fun as you get involved in a wide range of activities

- greater opportunities to get involved in volunteer work

- opportunities to work part-time on campus

- greater time off between academic years providing you with the opportunity to gain invaluable work experience or travel

- opportunities to study in other countries

- more opportunities to make
your own choices

- exposure to greater learning opportunities

- the opportunity for possible internships
in some fields of study

- the opportunity to be more challenged

- the opportunity to become independent

- the necessary requirements
for a future career

While I have likely forgotten a few things that could have been included in the above list, hopefully I have provided enough thoughts that you can now see that there are many advantages to attending a university. One final huge difference between high school and university that I would like to mention concerns financial matters.

For the most part in high school, most students never have to be concerned about financing their education as public high schools are free for most students in most countries. Although you might have had to pay for some supplies here or there, or for some field trips, for the most part you likely had help from your parents. College/university is a very different experience in this regard.

Most students (and their parents) are often shocked when they realize how much college/university will cost. Although there are various forms of government assistance and although your parents may be helping you (but not necessarily), it is still critical to budget your money regardless of where it is coming from. Some students drop out of school by the end of their first term or semester because they run out of the money that was supposed to last them for the complete school year. Other students, after graduating from college/university, sometimes have to work in menial jobs, completely unrelated to their area of studies, because they need to begin to pay back their student loans, and they can't afford to wait to find their dream job.

It is often said that money concerns contribute more to personal problems than any other single factor. Similarly, money problems can have a detrimental affect on your success. Learning how to manage your money in college/university is a skill that will be a huge benefit to you for the rest of your life. Although it is not within the scope of this book to provide a detailed overview of how to manage your money (I have written another book titled *Money Matters* that might be helpful to you), here are a few tips.

First of all, the key to financial success is spending less than you make. Rewording this for a college/university student, the key to financial success is spending less than you have. To do this, you need to calculate how much money you still have available after you pay for tuition, room/board, books, and other fees. You will then need to divide this amount of money by the number of weeks you will be at college/university during the school year. The result from this shows you how much you could spend each week in order to avoid running out of money before the school year ends. At the beginning of each week, you need to know exactly how much money you have available to spend, and at the end of each week you need to evaluate how you did. If you spend a little more than you budgeted during some weeks, then the following week, you need to spend a little less. If you are constantly running out of money, you need to become more self-disciplined in your spending or you could consider getting a part-time job.

v) KNOW WHERE TO GET HELP

At some time or another you are going to require some help during your studies. It might be that you need a map to find your classes during your first week of school. It might be that you need some help in choosing your courses. You might need help in purchasing your books. You might also need help to get a locker, a bus pass, information on clubs, information about medical assistance on campus, study skills, and on the list could go.

I will keep this simple. During orientation and your first week or two at college/university, keep a record of the various services that are available. Enter important campus phone numbers and email addresses into your cell phone.

There are a surprisingly number of staff members available at any college/university to help you. The key is for you become aware of these services before you actually require them.

vi) HAVE A REASON TO SUCCEED

College/university is hard work, even when you are in a program that you absolutely love. Success might be described as running in a marathon. On average, students spend three to four years at college/university. This is a long time, especially when you also consider the number of years you spent in school before arriving at university.

To help you complete your diploma or degree, you might find it useful to identify some benefits that you believe you will achieve by graduating from college/university. I often find that successful students have a very clear vision as to how graduating from university is going to help them. For many, graduating from college/university provides the qualifications for a job or even for future education.

For others, graduating provides a sense of pride. For some, graduating is the reward for hard work and persistence. For others, graduating will open the door for new opportunities. And finally for some, graduating is simply a concrete symbol to demonstrate their love of learning.

Whatever reasons you have for graduating, it can be helpful for you to write these down. I have worked with some students who created a success poster which showed various pictures of how they believe their life will be after they graduate from college/ university. Whichever technique you use, keep these words or images clearly before you. Whenever you are struggling with the amount of work you have to do or whenever you experience some aspect of failure, look at your list of reasons for wanting to graduate. If you have established a powerful list of ways in which you will benefit by graduating from university, these reasons can help to motivate you to be successful.

Jack Canfield and Mark Victor Hansen, two of the most successful authors during the past few decades, wrote, "The main reason most people struggle professionally and personally is simply a lack of focus." Whatever you are focusing on can play a direct role in your success, or your lack of success, at college/university.

vii) BELIEVE YOU CAN SUCCEED

Various successful people throughout history have stated something along the lines of: "You can if you believe you can." Of course, the opposite of this is true as well.

To be successful in anything you do in life, you have to believe that you can do it. Unfortunately, some students believe that college/university is going to be too hard for them, and in some cases give up before they really get going. If you can achieve the requirements to be accepted at a college/university, for most students it's not a matter of whether you have the ability to be successful; rather it is a matter of whether you have the right attitude (and work habits) to be successful.

It has been said that changing your attitude can change your altitude. To be successful, you must first believe that you will be successful. While this book is packed with tips and strategies to help you to be more successful, in the end these suggestions will matter very little if your mind is telling you that you can't be successful.

What we focus on is who we often become. What we think about the most generally directs our lives. Our mind can be like a steering wheel helping to direct us towards our goals, but it can also be a steering wheel turning us away from our goals. And most important, you are the person controlling the steering wheel.

It has often been said by experts in the field of thinking that most people tend to have far more negative thoughts each day than positive thoughts. For many students, the difference between success and failure is often directly related to their thoughts more than their abilities. Some intellectually gifted students fail to complete college/university because their thoughts sabotage any chance to be successful. On the other hand, some students with average ability achieve greatly in their studies because their "I can do it" attitude provided the fuel to succeed.

As you look at the tips in the remainder of this book, I suggest that you find two or three suggestions that you believe could make a positive difference for you. Write these thoughts on a piece of paper and carry them with you. Read them every morning and every night. Once these tips actually become part of your habits, browse through this book once again to see if you can find another suggestion or two that could increase your success even more. If so, once again constantly read these tips and attempt to live by them.

When you develop the appropriate habits of success, you will be successful beyond your dreams.

It is my hope that this book can help you to be more successful.

1. Take 100% responsibility for being successful. It is not up to anyone else other than you to achieve your dreams.

2. Before you attend the your new campus, spend some time surfing the college/university website. In particular look for services that are offered that might be beneficial to you.

3. Professors are there to help you. They want you to be successful. When in doubt, ask for help.

4. Plan on arriving so that you can participate in all orientation activities.

5. Set a regular time to communicate with your family.

6. It takes less time to fix a problem before it happens.

7. If you need to talk to a professor about an assignment, prepare some questions before your appointment.

8. Attend all your classes.

9. Nothing would ever get done if you had to first overcome every possible obstacle.

10. Exercise and good eating habits can
help you to be more successful.

11. Buy used texts to save money.

12. Being organized is like exercise. It's not very
effective if you only do it once in awhile.

13. When you have a goal you will
tend to be more successful.

14. Eliminate bad habits; repeat good habits.

15. When you choose your courses, carefully read the
course descriptions of all the courses
that are available to you.

16. If you have a roommate, establish some basic
rules such as a time for lights out, room
cleanliness, visitors, etc. Establish some rapport
with your roommate by focusing on common
interests rather than dwelling on your differences.

17. Ensure that your course selections are
completed by the stated deadlines.

18. Don't take more courses than you need during
your first year. There are no bonus marks or prizes
for taking more than you have to.

19. To be successful it is important to realize that for every hour you spend in class you should be doing at least 1 hour of related work outside of class (which can include assignments, projects, readings, preparing for your next class, and preparing for future tests).

20. Consider taking something completely different for some of your optional courses.

21. Most successful students take accurate notes in class.

22. Choose your courses carefully.

23. Before your first day of classes, walk to each of the buildings and locate your actual classrooms so that you will not be late on your first day of classes because you got lost.

24. Your chosen major should be based on both your interests and your abilities. In addition, match your major, if possible, to your eventual career field.

25. Don't keep your notes as loose papers . Either file them in a folder or keep them in a binder.

26. When you are choosing your courses you might find it helpful to go to the bookstore and peruse the required texts for any courses
you are considering taking.

27. Faster is not always better.

28. Spend most of your time with successful people.

29. Set a weekly budget and spend less each day than you intended.

30. The smallest step forward brings you closer to achieving your goals.

31. Locate your library before you begin your first day of classes.

32. Talk to other students about timesaving apps and also apps to help you be more organized (such as iStudiezPro, PocketList, EverNote, and Chegg).

33. If you find yourself constantly losing things, this is a warning that you need to find a way to better organize yourself.

34. Get a good night's sleep.

35. If you have a concern about a mark in a class,
consult with your professor in private,
not during your class.

36. Being organized can help to
reduce your level of stress.

37. Keep changing your actions until you get
the desired results.

38. The most successful students are those who work
consistently every day, rather than waiting until the
night before an assignment is due
or the night before a test before
they start to work.

39. Discover what services exist at your school
such as recreational, tutoring, and various help labs.

40. Never plagiarize.

41. Locate any cafeterias and all campus
restaurants before the first day of school.
If you have a meal plan, ensure that you
understand where you can eat and how often.

42. There is always a cost: understand the
demands of your time before you say
yes to any requests.

43. When you choose your courses,
have a backup plan.

44. After 2 or 3 classes, if the course is completely
different than what you were expecting, or the
professor's teaching style is alien to you, consider
changing this course to one in your backup plan.

45. If you want to get a higher mark, it is best to say,
"What can I do to improve my mark?" instead of
saying, "I need a higher mark." Show the professor
that you are willing to work harder to earn
a higher mark.

46. Lack of direction is often the real
reason for a lack of time.

47. The first step in achieving any goal
is to write it down.

48. Thank your professors for their feedback.
Learn from any criticism you receive.

49. If you need to drop a course, ensure that
you do it before the stated deadlines; otherwise
you might end up paying for the complete course.

50. If you are going in the wrong direction,
going faster still won't help you.

51. Before you begin any project,
ensure that you have all the required materials.

52. If you have the opportunity,
work as a research assistant for any professors
who are teaching in an area you would
like to major in.

53. If a personal problem is making
it difficult for you to be successful, make
an appointment to see
a counselor on your campus.

54. Ensure that you have the necessary prerequisites
for any courses that you choose.

55. Before you venture out on the campus at night,
be aware of volunteers or possible security
staff members who can accompany
you to ensure your safety.

56. Accept that everyone makes mistakes.

57. If you do poorly on your first few assignments,
don't get discouraged. Talk to your professor
about how you can improve. If necessary,
talk to someone on staff who helps with
student success.

58. If you don't understand something, ask for help.

59. If you have a financial need, make an appointment to see an advisor in the Financial Aid Office. There are often various forms of financial help for students with need.

60. If you are in a large class, attend all small group seminars related to the class.

61. There are times when it is necessary to move on to the next question even when you haven't finished the question before it.

62. When your professor posts a course outline (or syllabus) on your first day of class, keep this information in a safe place. It may include thoughts on how to be successful in this class as well as the professor's policies on attendance, lateness, and penalties for handing in late assignments. This information is critical to your success in any course. Read the information often, and highlight the important points. The handout will also likely include your course reading material. Even though a professor might not tell you what you should be reading each week, it is your responsibility to sort this out and do any

readings that are related to the current
topic that your professor is teaching.

63. You will be more successful if you do
your homework each day rather than leaving it
until the weekend to complete it in
a marathon session.

64. Whenever you find success,
keep repeating whatever you are doing.

65. Don't blame others when
things go wrong.

66. If everything is falling apart, talk to an advisor
about reducing your course load. It is generally
better to complete a few of your courses then
to throw them all away. In some courses you might
even be able to negotiate an "incomplete" and
then finish your course work over the summer.

67. Waking up 15 minutes earlier each day might help
you to have a more relaxing and productive day.

68. You will be more successful in completing large
assignments if you develop a plan and do a little
each day on them.

69. Clearly identify the problem before you

attempt to find some solutions.

70. Make a financial plan. Some students drop
out of college/university because they
run out of money. Budget wisely.

71. Be optimistic.

72. When you are given an assignment,
ensure that you understand exactly what you are
to do before you begin. If you have any confusion,
talk to your professor or his/her teaching assistant.
Waiting until the last minute to complete
an assignment could cause real problems for
you if there is something you don't understand and
you are unable to reach your professor for help.

73. Identify someone who is successful in the way
that you want to be successful and then
imitate whatever they do.

74. Focus on what is most important.

75. Make a list of reasons why you want to succeed.

76. When you study, you will be more successful if
you focus on one subject area for several hours rather
than changing subjects every 10-15 minutes.

77. In completing any task the single most
important word to remember is "action".

78. The best way to handle "test stress"
is to be overly prepared.

79. Go for a walk.

80. Find a reason to talk to your professor one-to-one
so that he/she knows who you are and
also knows that you are serious about learning
(and you are interested in the content
of this class).

81. Plan your studying for an exam so that you get a
good night's sleep before the exam.

82. Get involved in activities that
are offered on your campus.

83. Instead of thinking about what you have to do
next, focus on what you are doing right now.

84. Successful people build on their strengths.

85. Professors often provide hints or clues
as to what is going to be on an exam. Listen
carefully throughout the course for any
topics that are emphasized.

86. Studying is about how much you learn, rather than how many hours you study. Learn study techniques that can help you to be more successful. These could include learning to highlight important parts of your notes. These could also include using practice tests (you can even make your own with friends) and writing out the answers. The worst way to study is to simply read your notes and texts. Effective studying requires you to write and/or state your learning in response to sample questions.

87. Generally the same old ways achieve the same old results.

88. Clubs that you join can help you to meet new friends. They can also help you to establish contacts which might someday be beneficial to you as you seek employment after graduating.

89. If you find yourself getting overwhelmed, there is a counseling department on campus that can direct you to someone who can help you to be better organized and deal more positively with stress.

90. When you are studying, turn off your cell phone.

91. Some people study better
listening to music; others don't. It is important
to understand what works best for you.

92. Let others help you.

93. Along with well-organized notes, keep all tests
(with correct answers). These materials can form the
foundation of your study resources for your exams.

94. At the beginning of each day, identify what you
want to accomplish during the day.

95. Discuss your course requirements with
an advisor. When selecting your courses,
ensure that you are taking any compulsory
courses that you require for graduation
in your program.

96. Students don't generally plan
to fail; sometimes they just fail to plan.

97. Finding the best in others will help
them to find the best in you.

98. If you have to complete a group project, choose
the best people you can find to be your partners.

99. Successful people are persistent.

100. When you receive a test or
assignment back from your professor, ensure
that you know the correct answers or what
you could have done to achieve a better mark.

101. Pace yourself.

102. Network with people who share your
interests, whether these are staff members
or other students.

103. Schedule your most important tasks for the
time of the day when you know you
are the most productive.

104. Eating well can increase
success in all areas of your life.

105. There is a tendency to become the average of
the people you spend most of your time with.

106. Generally, it takes less time to do a job today
then it does to postpone it until tomorrow.

107. Always be early for class.

108. Read to understand, not just to memorize.

109. Always back up your computer files.

110. Verifying the details of anything you
have to do can be a timesaver and help
you to be more successful.

111. At times, school can be stressful. Understand
which strategies and techniques work best
for you in dealing with stress.

112. If you are struggling in a class, there may be
remedial help, extra seminars, and tutoring
possibilities to help you.

113. Never cheat.

114. During a lecture you should constantly
be taking notes, although it is also important to
participate. Strong notes are often the key
to being successful in preparing for exams.

115. Success rarely happens overnight.

116. If you are given any readings
before a class, do them. This will increase
your learning during the lecture.

117. Eat a slow, nutritious breakfast.

118. There are likely people, such as your parents,
who may have played a significant role

in helping you to reach college/university;
don't forget about them now that you
are living apart from them.

119. Learn to ignore your negative thoughts
in the same way you might ignore
someone who is pestering you.

120. Every once in awhile, push yourself
beyond your comfort zone.

121. The main job is always to
keep the main job the main job.

122. Introduce yourself to your professors.

123. When you answer a question in class, remind
everyone of your name until your professor
calls you by your name.

124. Enter any emergency call numbers for
your university campus into your cell phone.

125. If you are working hard but not getting
very good results, you might need to change
the way you are working.

126. Review your class notes each day after class.
Highlight anything you think could be important.

You could even begin to write study cards or
form a list of questions that you think might
appear on an exam.

127. The key points in any lecture often occur
at the beginning of a lecture and in the
summary at the end. Don't be late for class
and don't be in a rush to leave
as class is ending.

128. Taking a day to rest when you are
beginning to feel sick may be better than trying
to attend all your classes and then missing
a week because you get really sick.

129. There's a time to work and a time to play;
strive for a balance in your life.

130. Have a friend in each of your classes who can
tell you what you missed if you are ever sick,
and do the same for them as well..

131. If there are any extra seminars, assignments, or
rewriting tests you can do to achieve
additional marks, do them.

132. Sometimes what you think you have to
do is more tiring than what you
actually have to do.

133. School is demanding; don't make it more difficult by using/abusing drugs and alcohol.

134. Form a study group to ask each other questions.

135. Have others proof your work before you hand it in.

136. Whenever you have a presentation to make, practice the presentation in front of someone else who can time you and provide some feedback.

137. Avoid negative people.

138. You will never know if you don't try.

139. Don't make the same mistake twice.

140. Prioritize what you have to do and start with your most important tasks.

141. If you are making a class presentation, arrive early to ensure that your audio visual equipment is working.

142. Talk to the person who is most likely to make things happen for you.

143. Be enthusiastic.

144. If you love what you are doing,
it will be easier to be successful.

145. Have a written list of things you have
to complete each day and review the list often.

146. Avoid junk food and drinks
with a high sugar content.

147. Have a specific place where you always put those
"little things" like your keys, wallet/purse, etc.

148. Relax.

149. Keep eliminating what doesn't work
until you find what does.

150. The first step is always just that.

151. Praise others in public;
resolve conflicts in private.

152. If you can't change what you would like to
change, maybe you need to change your
attitude towards it.

153. Action is the key to success.

154. Place time limits on any task you are working on.

155. A few minutes at the end of each day organizing yourself for tomorrow will usually take less time than if you save the same task for the morning.

156. Take one minute mental vacations.

157. Avoid loaning money to friends because you might end up with neither.

158. Solve your own problems before you try to rescue everyone else.

159. If you are taking an online course, keep in mind that the professor can access how many times you have logged into the course, how much of the course content you are reading, and how many times you reply to others or to the professor. If you rarely log into your course and rarely get involved in any discussions this information will be available to your professor as he evaluates your work in the course.

160. Spend most of your time with those who bring out the best in you.

161. You don't have to stay up at night to be successful; you just have to stay awake during the day.

162. What will your life look like 5 years from now? What can you do today to take one step towards making this happen?

163. Reward yourself for working hard.

164. Set a specific time to do your homework.

165. Keep up on your readings each day.

166. While you should attempt to attend all your classes, this is even more critical in the week before your exams when professors may review what is important or drop some hints as to key areas that you should be studying.

167. Prepare study notes throughout your course instead of waiting until exam time.

168. If the teaching assistants for any of your classes provide review sessions leading up to your exams, then attend all the sessions and carefully listen for what they consider to be important.

169. Plan on getting at least 8 hours of sleep the night before any of your exams.

170. Winning is the result of developing

certain habits; unfortunately so is losing.

171. Strive to be more in control
of yourself and less in control of others.

172. The library may have archives of old exams
in your course that you can use to practice.

173. Deadlines are usually less threatening
after you have taken the first step in reaching them.

174. When you write an exam, plan your time
so that you don't end up spending too much
time on one question which could result in
you not completing the exam.

175. Good luck is often the result of
good preparation.

176. If you want to change your life,
begin by changing your attitude.

177. Pay attention to the details.

178. Form a clear picture of what you
want to achieve.

179. On any test, answer the question that has
been asked. You won't help yourself if you

go in an entirely different direction in
an attempt to show how much you have learned.
As you write your answer constantly reread
the question to ensure that you are answering it.

180. Focus on one task at a time.

181. There are times when handing an assignment
in on time, even though it is not perfect, is better
than trying to make it perfect and handing it in late.

182. Sit near the front of your class.

183. Whenever you are answering a question,
support your thoughts with quotes and references
from your texts and class notes. Being specific
creates a stronger answer than being general.

184. If you don't do as well as you were expecting on
an assignment, ask your professor how you could
do better next time.

185. Of all the terrible things that you think might
happen, only a few might ever really occur, and
sometimes none of them.

186. There are no bonus marks for being
the first person to finish an exam.
Stay to the end and reread every question

and proof all your answers.

187. Always keep sight of the bigger picture while being content with smaller achievements.

188. Do it right the first time.

189. You will generally be more productive if you keep your schedule somewhere else than in your head.

190. Set weekly goals.

191. Record all upcoming assignments and tests on a calendar that you look at every day.

192. When faced with large projects, find a way to break the project into small manageable steps. Then establish a timeline for completing each step.

193. Always have others proof your essays. Don't depend on "spell check" and/or "grammar check" to find all your errors.

194. If your professor (or teacher assistant) goes out of his/her way to help you with an assignment or some other question you might have had, send them a thank you

note to express your gratitude.

195. Complete a draft for any assignment before you begin your good copy.

196. Let your professor know that you are interested and that you want to learn. You can do this by sitting near the front of your class, ensuring the professor knows your name, and by asking questions and participating in discussions. Professors enjoy teaching students who can actually demonstrate that they have read the materials that were assigned for class.

197. Emphasize quality, not quantity.

198. It's easier to increase your speed when you know exactly where you are going.

199. Keep a master list of everything you have to do.

200. Strive for excellence.

201. Pursue your passion.

About the Author

Brian Harris is an award-winning teacher/counselor and best-selling author. He has extensive experience in assisting people with their career planning as well as helping students and adults to find life success. He has also achieved the designation of International Professional Speaker.

Brian lives in Burlington, Canada, with his wife and two teenage daughters. In addition to writing, Brian is a part-time lecturer in counseling at Queen's University. He is also an accomplished artist (www.bcharris.com).

Brian enjoys family trips and is an avid canoeist and scuba diver.

Additional information about Brian can be found at
www.cgscommunications.com